MW00983432

A New Creation

2 Corinthians 5:17

A Study Guide for
the New Believer

New Believers Fellowship

CALVARY CHAPEL COSTA MESA

All Scripture quotations in this book are taken from the King James Version of the Bible.

A New Creation

Copyright © 2000 by Calvary Chapel Costa Mesa

Published by Calvary Chapel Costa Mesa

ISBN 0-9700218-3-6

All Rights Reserved. No part of this publication may be reproduced, stored in a retrieval system, or transmitted in any form or by any means without the express written consent of the author.

Printed in the United States of America

It is our desire that as you utilize the material in this book that you will become equipped and have an understanding of many of the foundations of the Christian faith. Today, more than ever before, we need to be *"Rooted and built up in Him, and established in the faith"* (Colossians 2:7). With this goal set before us, let's run the race to win.

Contained in this book are fourteen lessons that, if diligently studied, will provide you with a good beginning foundation to a faith that will guide you through life's good and stormy times. It is our hope that as you apply these Biblical principles to your life, that you will be as the one whom Jesus said: *"Therefore whosoever heareth these sayings of Mine, and doeth them, I will liken him unto a wise man, which built his house upon a rock: And the rain descended, and the floods came, and the winds blew, and beat upon that house; and it fell not: for it was founded upon a rock"* (Matthew 7:24-25). Jesus is that Rock.

James tells us *"Draw nigh to God and He will draw nigh to you"* (James 4:8). This is our hope and prayer for you who have come to trust in Jesus Christ and desire to make Him Lord of your life.

In His Grace,

Tim Fraser

Repentance & Faith

REPENTANCE

To repent means to change your mind and attitude about sin. It means to turn from your sin and turn to God (Jesus Christ) for forgiveness and cleansing.

1. WHO PREACHED THE NEED FOR REPENTANCE?

a. Matthew 3:2 _John the Baptist_

b. Matthew 4:17 _Jesus_

c. Mark 6:7-12 _Jesus + disciples_

d. Acts 2:38 _Peter_

e. Acts 17:22 & 30 _Paul_

2. WHAT ARE THE CHARACTERISTICS OF TRUE REPENTANCE?

a. 2 Corinthians 7:9-10 _sorrow_

b. Luke 18:9-14 _being humbled_

c. 1 Thessalonians 1:9 _turn away from idols_

3. REPENTANCE IS A CHANGE OF 3 ELEMENTS:

a. *Intellectual element* – a change of mind, of what we think.

b. *Emotional element* – a change of heart, of what we desire.

c. *Volitional element* – a change of will, of what we do.

4. WHAT IS TO BE OUR MESSAGE TO THE WORLD?

Luke 24:45-48 *There is forgiveness to all who turn to Jesus.*

FAITH

1. HOW DOES THE BIBLE DEFINE FAITH?

Hebrews 11:1 *Confidence that what we hope for will happen!*

2. HOW WOULD YOU DEFINE FAITH?

Believing in what we can't see.

3. WHERE DOES FAITH COME FROM?

Hebrews 12:2 *Keeping our eyes on Jesus*

4. HOW DO WE RECEIVE OUR FAITH?

Romans 10:17 *listening to the Goodness of God*

5. THE IMPORTANCE OF FAITH:

a. We are saved by it – Ephesians 2:8-9.

b. We live by it – 2 Corinthians 5:7.

c. It is our shield against the enemy – Ephesians 6:16.

d. It never gives up – Hebrews 11:7 & 30.

e. It gives us victory over the world and its problems – 1 John 5:4-5.

The principle element in repentance is a change of mind and attitude about Christ; a change from an unbelieving and rejecting attitude to a believing and accepting attitude. *True*

6

faith in Christ involves the confession and forsaking of sin. *True repentance and faith* are inseparable. They are mutually dependent upon each other.

Application Question: How have I repented and trusted Christ?

_____

_____

_____

_____

Assignment: Read John 1, memorize John 1:12-13, and pray for one another.

Notes/Questions: But, to all who believed him + accepted him, he gave the right to become children of God. They are reborn! This is not a physical birth resulting from human passion or plan — this rebirth comes from God.

Sin, Salvation and Forgiveness

How was your faith put into action this week? _____

_____

SIN

1. WHAT IS SIN?

    a. Romans 3:23 _falling short of God's standards_

    b. Isaiah 53:6 _left God's path_

    c. 1 John 3:4 _opposes the law of God_

2. WHO SINS?

    a. 1 Kings 8:46 _everyone_

    b. Romans 3:23 _all_

    c. 1 John 1:8 _all_

3. WHERE DID SIN COME FROM?

    a. Isaiah 14:12-15 _Satan_

    b. Romans 5:12 _Adam's sin brought death_

4. WHY DO I SIN?

    a. Adam's decision in the Garden of Eden:

        1) God told Adam not to eat of the Tree of the Knowledge of Good and Evil (Genesis 2).

        2) Sin in the human race originated in Adam's free decision to disobey the will of God (Genesis 3).

    b. The effects of Adam's decision on us today:

        1) Sin entered the world through one man, Adam (Romans 5:12).

        2) Adam's sin separated man from God (Genesis 3:22).

        3) Adam's sin resulted in both physical and spiritual death for mankind:

            a) Physical death – separation of the soul from the body (Genesis 3:19).

            b) Spiritual death – separation of the soul from God for eternity (Romans 6:23, 2 Thessalonians 1:8-10).

SALVATION

1. THE DEFINITION OF SALVATION:

It is being saved from the power and dominion of sin in our life, and from an eternity separated from God.

2. WHAT IS GOD'S GIFT TO US?

John 3:16 & Romans 6:23 *eternal life*

3. HOW ARE YOU SAVED?

Ephesians 2:8-9 *gift from God*

4. WHO DO WE PUT OUR FAITH IN FOR SALVATION?

Romans 10:9-10 & 13 *Jesus, God, Lord*

FORGIVENESS

1. THE DEFINITION OF FORGIVENESS:

It is to give up all claim to punish or exact penalty for an offense, to overlook.

a. What does God want to do with your sin? 1 John 1:9

forgive us and cleanse us

b. What must we be willing to do? Matthew 6:14-15

forgive others

c. How does God now see my sin? Jeremiah 31:34

He does not remember it

2. WHAT IS OUR RESPONSE TO GOD'S GIFT OF SALVATION?

Read Ephesians 2:10

To do the good things God has planned.

Assignment: Read Ephesians 2, memorize Ephesians 2:8-9, and pray for one another.

Notes/Questions: *God saved you by his special favor when you believed. And you can't take credit for this, it is a gift from God. Salvation is not a reward for the good things we have done so none of us can boast about it.*

11

The Word of God, Part 1

What difference did forgiveness from God make in your life this week? _____

_____

_____

THE WORD OF GOD, PART 1

1. DEFINITION:

The Bible is God's revelation of Himself to man, His creation. The Bible forms one continuous story, the story of humanity in relation to God. The Bible has one great theme: the person and work of Jesus Christ.

2. GOD'S WORD IS A PROGRESSIVE REVELATION:

Read Hebrews 1:1-3 and see how God has spoken:

    a. Distinct times

    b. Various manners

    c. Times past

    d. Unto the fathers by the prophets

    e. In these last days

    f. Unto us in His Son (the express image of His person)

3. THE BIBLE IS A SPECIAL BOOK:

Read 2 Timothy 3:16-17:

    a. What portion of Scripture is inspired (or "God breathed") by God? _____ ALL _____

Note: Inspired means "God breathed."

    b. What is God's word profitable for?

      1) teach us what is true

      2) realize what is wrong in our li[fe]

      3) Straightens us out &

      4) teaches us to do what is right

    c. According to verse 17, what does Scripture equip us to do? for every good thing God wants us to do.

4. CHARACTERISTICS OF THE WORD OF GOD:

    a. The Word of God is:

      1 Peter 1:23-25 the Good news

    b. The Word is:

      Hebrews 4:12 full of living power

    c. The Word will:

      Luke 21:33 remain forever

    d. The Word is:

      Romans 1:16 power

    ("The Word" here means the same as "the gospel.")

    e. The Word will never;

      Isaiah 55:11 be fruitless

5. HOW DO I KNOW I CAN TRUST THE BIBLE ?

a. 2 Peter 1:20-21 assures us that God's Word is true and reliable. (Note: There are over 300 prophecies in the Old Testament fulfilled during the life and ministry of Jesus. If we analyze the probability of one person fulfilling just 8, the probability would be 1 in 10 with 17 zeros after it! We can understand why Peter declares that the written word of prophecy is *more sure.*)

b. 2 Timothy 3:16 tells us that all Scripture finds its origin in God.

c. Titus 1:2 tells us that God cannot lie.

d. What does this say about the reliability of God's Word?

Assignment: Read Psalm 119:1-88, memorize Psalm 119:16, and pray for one another.

Notes/Questions: _____

_____

_____

_____

The Word of God, Part 2

Can you say as the Psalmist, "*I will delight myself in Thy statutes: I will not forget Thy Word.*" (Psalm 119:16)? _____

THE WORD OF GOD, PART 2

1. AN OVERVIEW OF THE BIBLE:

a. The Bible contains 66 books; 39 in the Old Testament and 27 in the New Testament.

b. The books are divided into chapters and verses for our reference (these were added later for our benefit and are not inspired).

c. The Old Testament was written in the Hebrew language.

d. The New Testament was written in the Greek language. (Remember that our English Bible is a translation from these original languages.)

e. Why is there a need for a New Testament? What is wrong with the Old Testament? Read Hebrews 8:9-10.

　　1) The foundation of the old covenant (or testament) with Israel was based on man's obedience to God.

　　2) The foundation of the new covenant is God's action on behalf of man. (Note the "I wills" in verse 10. It was enacted by the shed blood of Jesus Christ (Luke 22:20).

2. HOW TO STUDY THE SCRIPTURES:

Read Isaiah: 28:9-13:

a. Precept upon precept: a precept is an *established fact* of God's Word, i.e., "all have sinned"; "God is love"; "Jesus has risen".

b. Line upon line: the systematic story line of Scripture that ties the established facts of God together.

c. Here a little, there a little: the use of the foundational facts of Scripture to understand the other portions of Scripture.

Note: the New Testament is contained in the Old Testament and that the Old Testament is explained in the New Testament.

3. BECAUSE THE BIBLE IS INSPIRED, WE NEED THE HELP OF THE HOLY SPIRIT TO HELP US UNDERSTAND IT:

a. The man without the Spirit does not understand the things that come from God – 1 Corinthians 2:14.

b. The Holy Spirit will teach us and help us to remember – John 14:26.

4. ONE METHOD OF STUDYING GOD'S WORD IS GIVEN BELOW. THERE ARE OTHERS:

Turn to Mark 4:35-41 and read the passage. Now answer the following questions from these verses:

a. *Who?* What is being said about the person(s) involved? What does the person say? _____

_____

b. *What?* What is happening? What are the events? In what order are the events occurring? _____

_____

c. *Where?* Where is the event taking place? Where are people coming from or going to? _____

_____

d. *When?* When did the events take place? _____

_____

e. *Why?* Why is this story included? Why is it here in the text? Why does one person say what he does?

_____

f. *Wherefore? So what?* What difference would it make in my life if I were to apply this truth? _____

_____

Application Question: How much time should I spend in a week reading and studying my Bible?_____

_____

_____

Assignment: Read Psalm 119:89-176, memorize Psalm 119:105, and pray for one another.

Notes/Questions: _____

_____

_____

_____

God the Father

How important is the Word of God to you? Could it change your life? _____

_____

GOD THE FATHER

1. THE EXISTENCE OF GOD:

    a. The Bible does not seek to prove the existence of God. The fact that there is a God is taught throughout the Scriptures. The first verse of the Bible, Genesis 1:1, is an example: *In the beginning God created the heaven and the earth.* God's existence is presented as a statement of fact that needs no proof. The man who says there is no God is called a fool in Psalm 14:1.

    b. However, even apart from the Bible, there are certain evidences for the existence of God.

        1) Mankind has always believed in a universal being.

        2) We know that creation must have a creator. The universe could not originate without a first cause.

        3) The wonderful design which we see in creation demands an infinite designer.

        4) Since man is an intelligent being, his creator must have been of a much higher order in order to create him.

2. THE NATURE OF GOD:

    a. God is Spirit – He is invisible:

        1) John 1:18 _____

        2) John 4:24 _____

    b. God is a person. Personal names are used in reference to Him:

        1) Exodus 3:14 _____

        2) Exodus 6:3 _____

3. THE ATTRIBUTES (CHARACTERISTICS) OF GOD:

    a. Omnipresent (He is present everywhere) – Jeremiah 23:23-24.

    b. Omnipotent (He is all powerful)– Jeremiah 32:17 & 27.

    c. Omniscient (He is all knowing) – Job 34:21.

    d. Eternal (He is everlasting) – Deuteronomy 33:27.

    e. Holy (He is free from defilement, absolutely pure) – Isaiah 6:3.

    f. Righteous or just (He always does what is right) – Psalm 145:17.

    g. Merciful (He does not give us what we deserve) – Deuteronomy 4:31.

    h. Faithful (trustworthy, He will not let you down) – Deuteronomy 7:9.

    i. Immutable (He does not change) – Malachi 3:6.

    j. Awesome (He fills us with profound reverence, worthy of reverence and solemn respect)– Deuteronomy 7:21.

    k. Personal characteristics are ascribed to Him:

        1) Knowledge – Isaiah 55:8-10.

        2) Emotions – Genesis 6:6.

3) Will – Joshua 3:9-10.

4. THE LOVE OF GOD:

    a. What is the very essence of His nature? 1 John 4:7-8 & 16

    b. Whom does God love?

        1) Matthew 3:17 _____

        2) John 3:16 _____

    c. How did God demonstrate His love for us? Romans 5:8

_____

    d. How do I experience God's love each day? Romans 5:5

_____

5. THE FATHER IS GOD:

The Father holds the *place of authority* within the Godhead. He is not more important than the Son or the Holy Spirit but authorizes their ministries – John 6:38 and 14:16.

Assignment: Read John 8, memorize 1 John 1:3, and pray for one another.

Notes/Questions: _____

_____

_____

_____

Jesus the Son

Are your able to call God the Father "Papa" or "Daddy"? (see Romans 8:15) _____

JESUS THE SON

1. **JESUS POSSESSES ALL OF THE ATTRIBUTES OF GOD:**

   a. Omnipresent – Matthew 28:18-20.

   b. Omnipotent – Matthew 28:18.

   c. Omniscient – John 16:30.

   d. Eternal – John 1:1-2.

   e. Holy – Acts 3:14.

   f. Creator – Colossians 1:16-17.

   g. Faithful – 2 Thessalonians 3:3.

   h. Merciful – Jude 21.

2. **JESUS IS CALLED GOD IN THE NEW TESTAMENT:**

   a. John 10:29-33 _____

   b. John 20:28 _____

   c. Who is called God in Hebrews 1:8? _____

3. THE UNIQUENESS OF JESUS:

(Webster's definition of unique – "being the only one".)

    a. Unique in His virgin birth:

        1) Prophesied in Isaiah 7:14.

        2) Fulfilled in Matthew 1:18-25.

    b. Unique in His sinless life – Hebrews 4:14-16.

    c. Unique in His death:

        1) Why did He die? 1 Peter 3:18

_____

_____

        2) He was separated from the Father for the first time – Matthew 27:46.

    d. Unique in His resurrection from the dead:

        1) It is recorded in the Bible – Matthew 28, Mark 16, Luke 24, and John 20 & 21.

        2) He was witnessed by over 500 people – 1 Corinthians 15:1-8.

        3). Because of His power over death and sin, we too have spiritual power in our lives – 1 Corinthians 15:12-14 & 56 and Romans 5:10.

        4) The Christian faith rests on His resurrection – 1 Corinthians 15:17.

4. CHRIST DESIRES US TO LIVE OUR LIFE THROUGH HIM:

Read Galatians 2:20 to answer these two questions:

    a. Who lives in us once we have become believers?

_____

b. How do you think this might change your life?

_____

_____

5. THE ONLY LIFE THAT PLEASED THE FATHER WAS THAT OF HIS SON:

a. Who are we to listen to? Luke 9:35 _____

_____

b. Who is the Way to the Father? John 14:6 _____

_____

Application Question: What attribute of Jesus do you find most powerful?

_____

_____

_____

Assignment: Read John 3-4, memorize John 3:16, and pray for one another.

Notes/Questions: _____

_____

_____

_____

Assurance

Can you say that you know Jesus the Son of God better this week? _____

_____

_____

ASSURANCE

We are assured and certain of our salvation because of the authority of God's Word. There are many evidences we can look at to know we are saved and have eternal life.

1. GOD PROMISES ETERNAL LIFE IN HIS WORD:

  a. According to John 1:12, what is the promise associated with receiving Jesus?_____

  _____

  b. John 3:16 states that whoever believes in Jesus has:

  _____

  c. John 5:24 says that the one who believes in God will not experience: _____

  d. In John 10:27-28 we learn that we will never:

  _____

  _____

2. THE HOLY SPIRIT GIVES US ASSURANCE OF OUR SALVATION:

    a. According to Romans 8:16-17, what does the Holy Spirit bear witness of in our lives?_____

_____

    b. What is the guarantee of our future life according to Ephesians 1:13-14?_____

3. TURN TO THE BOOK OF 1 JOHN. WHAT IS THE PURPOSE OF JOHN'S LETTER AS STATED IN 1 JOHN 5:13?

_____

_____

_____

The Apostle John uses the phrase "we know" (we have an assurance) more than 30 times throughout his letter to help these believers come to a place of assurance about their salvation. This letter is considered to be the best explanation of how we as believers can truly know that our salvation is real.

    a. According to 1 John 2:3-5, how do we know for sure that we *know Him*? _____

    b. In 1 John 2:21-23, what is the action here that rules out any assurance of salvation? _____

_____

    c. What is the basis of assurance in 1 John 3:14-15?

_____

    d. In 1 John 4:13, what has God given to His children to bring us assurance of our salvation? _____

_____

e. According to 1 John 4:14-15, what work does the Spirit produce in us that brings assurance?

_____

_____

4. GOD IS THE ONE WHO DOES THE WORK:

a. Philippians 1:3-6 tells us that God has begun *this good work* in us.

b. How long will He continue in *this good work*?

_____

God wants you and I to know that we have eternal life (1 John 5:11-13). It is not His will that we live our life wondering daily if we are saved. If you doubt your salvation remember that our salvation rests only on God's finished work for us. Even if our hearts at times forget that, it is still true (1 John 3:19-20). Pray and ask God to remind you of His faithfulness to keep His promises.

Assignment: Read 1 John, memorize Philippians 1:6, and pray for one another.

Notes/Questions: _____

_____

_____

_____

Prayer

Why should we always be thankful for God's Word? _____

_____

"Everyone engages in prayer at one time or another. Even that person who says, "I don't believe in God," cries out when the crisis looms, "Oh God, help me!" We are all acquainted with prayer to some extent or another. Prayer is one of the greatest privileges God has given man. We can come into the presence of God, the Creator of this universe, and talk with Him. And what's more, He always listens!"

Chuck Smith in *Effective Prayer Life*, page 49

PRAYER

1. WHAT IS PRAYER? _____

_____

_____

2. WHO SHOULD PRAY?

Psalm 32:6 _____

3. TO WHOM SHOULD WE PRAY?

Matthew 6:5-15 _____

4. WHAT SHOULD WE PRAY ABOUT?

a. Philippians 4:6 _____

b. Matthew 6:10 _____

c. Matthew 9:38 _____

d. 2 Thessalonians 3:1_____

e. James 5:13-16 _____

f. Ephesians 3:14-19 _____

5. WHERE SHOULD WE PRAY?

a. 1 Corinthians 1:2_____

b. Luke 19:46_____

c. Matthew 6:6 _____

6. WHEN SHOULD WE PRAY?

a. Luke 18:1 _____

b. 1 Thessalonians 3:10 _____

c. Psalm 61:2_____

7. WHY SHOULD WE PRAY?

a. Luke 22:40_____

b. Ephesians 6:10-12 & 18 _____

c. Ephesians 3:14-20 _____

d. John 15:5 _____

8. HOW SHOULD WE PRAY?

a. Romans 8:26 _____

b. 1 John 5:14 _____

c. Jude 20 _____

d. 1 Corinthians 14:15 _____

9. HINDRANCES IN PRAYER

    a. Isaiah 59:2 _____

    b. James 1:6-8 _____

    c. James 4:3 _____

    d. Luke 18:9-14 _____

Assignment: Read Ephesians 1:15-23 and 3:14-21, memorize James 5:16, and pray for one another.

Notes/Questions: _____

_____

_____

_____

Satan and Spiritual Warfare

What keeps our prayers from being answered? _____

SATAN AND SPIRITUAL WARFARE

1. HIS NAMES GIVE US INSIGHT INTO HIS EVIL CHARACTER:

a. "Satan" is his most frequently used name – it is used more than 50 times – it means "adversary" or "opponent".

b. The name Devil is used more than 30 times – it means "slanderer".

c. John 8:44 _____

d. 2 Corinthians 4:4 _____

e. 2 Corinthians 11:13-15 _____

f. Ephesians 2:2 _____

g. 1 Thessalonians 3:5 & Matthew 4:3 _____

h. Revelation 9:11 _____

i. Revelation 12:10 _____

2. HOW DOES SATAN OPERATE?

   a. Ephesians 6:11 _____

   b. 1 Peter 5:8-9 _____

   c. John 8:44 _____

   d. Genesis 3:13 and Revelation 20:10 _____

   _____

3. BUT WHAT DID JESUS COME TO DO ACCORDING TO 1 JOHN 3:8? _____

SPIRITUAL WARFARE

1. WE STAND STRONG IN THE LORD AND IN THE POWER OF HIS MIGHT – EPHESIANS 6:10-18 TELLS US HOW.

2. PUT ON THE FULL ARMOR OF GOD (ALL OF IT):

   a. *The belt of truth* – Truth overcomes deceit and lies. It equips us to walk uprightly in our Christian lives.

   b. *The breastplate of righteousness* – This speaks of right acts practiced by the believer. The breastplate protects the heart of the soldier (See 2 Timothy 2:4).

   c. *The sandals of the gospel* – The sandals speak of mobility and preparedness. We are to be ready to use God's Word in spiritual battles (See also 1 Peter 3:15).

   d. *The shield of faith* – The shield protects us from the attacks (those fiery darts) of Satan (e.g., temptations, impure thoughts). Above all take up this weapon.

   e. *The helmet of salvation* – It refers to the intake of the Word of God which will help protect our thoughts from doubt, the world, the flesh and the devil. It will make us secure in our relationship with the Lord.

   f. *The sword which is the Word of God* – This is our

only offensive weapon. When we are attacked, we are to respond with the Word of God.

3. REALIZE THAT IT IS NOT A PHYSICAL BATTLE, IT IS SPIRITUAL:

Read 2 Corinthians 10:3-7.

a. What can spiritual weapons accomplish?

_____

_____

_____

4. HOW DID JESUS RESPOND TO SATAN'S ATTACKS?

a. Read Matthew 4:1-11 and answer these questions:

1) What was the physical condition of Jesus?

_____

2) What was the response of Jesus to Satan's three offers?

a) _____

b) _____

c) _____

3) What does this tell us about handling temptation or trials of any kind? _____

_____

5. WHAT IS THE PROMISE OF 1 JOHN 4:4?

_____

_____

_____

Assignment: Read Matthew 4 and Jude, memorize Ephesians 6:12, and pray for one another.

Notes/Questions: _____

_____

_____

_____

Putting Christ First

How did 1 John 4:4 minister to you this week?_____

_____

_____

PUTTING CHRIST FIRST

1. DEFINITION OF LORDSHIP:

The Lordship of Jesus Christ is the daily submission and surrender of our entire self to the authority and leadership of Jesus Christ, recognizing His sovereign right to rule over us. Read and consider 2 Corinthians 5:14-15 and Colossians 1:18.

2. WHAT IS JESUS' PLAN FOR HIS DISCIPLES?

a. Luke 9:23 states the heart of discipleship:
If anyone wants to follow Jesus and become His disciple he must:

1) _____

Putting the Lord and others first, and refusing to live my life to please myself.

2) _____

Taking up your cross daily: submitting our will to the will of God. Jesus did - read Luke 22:42.

3) _____

Following Jesus and no one or nothing else. Read Matthew 4:19 and 1 Peter 2:21 for more insight.

b. The whole principle of Lordship is the removal of self from the throne of our lives and the invitation to Jesus to sit on that throne and rule, trusting Him to do what is best for us.

c. The battle of submission: There are two reasons why people do not acknowledge Jesus Christ as Lord of their life:

    1) We are afraid God may ask us to do something we do not want to do.

    2) We are not sure that God has our best interest at heart.

    3) Yet, consider Jeremiah 29:11-14.

3. HOW DO I KNOW IF CHRIST IS LORD OF MY LIFE?

a. According to John 14:15, 21 & 23, we show our love for Jesus by: _____

b. James 1:22-25 tells us that I must read the Word of God, see what God's will is for my life and then:

_____

4. HOW DO OTHERS KNOW IF CHRIST IS LORD OF MY LIFE?

a. What does John 13:35 say is the mark of a disciple of Jesus? _____

5. WHAT IS THE BLESSING OF PUTTING CHRIST FIRST IN MY LIFE?

a. 1 Peter 3:15-16 _____

b. Romans 12:1-2 _____

c. Romans 6:22 _____

The Lordship of Jesus Christ is the most crucial issue of any Christian's life. We are all aware of those around us who are reaping the by-products of their lack of obedience. Jesus has our best interests at heart. We must give Him our entire life and we must live only for Him daily. Only then will we experience the full life that He has promised us. As we continually confess Jesus Christ as Lord of our lives, we are assured of true faith living in our hearts. Read and consider Romans 10:9-13.

Application Question: What keeps me from totally letting Jesus run my life?

_____

_____

_____

_____

Assignment: Read Romans 7 and 8, memorize Matthew 16:24, and pray for one another.

Notes/Questions: _____

_____

_____

_____

Fellowship

What does it mean to be a follower of Jesus? _____

_____

_____

FELLOWSHIP

1. DEFINITION:

Fellowship is sharing with others in a deep, personal way. It is a friendly association of people with similar interests and tastes..

2. THE DISTINCTION BETWEEN THE BELIEVER AND THE WORLD:

Read 1 Peter 2:9-11 and answer these four questions:

a. What names does Peter call us in verse 9?

_____

_____

_____

b. Have we always been His people according to verse 10?

_____

c. How are we described in this present world by verse 11?

_____

d. What should be our response? (verse 11)

_____

3. WITH WHOM DO WE FELLOWSHIP?

a. 2 Corinthians 13:14 _____

b. 1 John 1:3 _____

c. 1 John 1:7 _____

4. WHAT IS OUR MOTIVATION TO FELLOWSHIP?

a. Romans 8:35-39 _____

b. 1 John 2:3-6 _____

c. Hebrews 10:24-25 _____

5. THE ACTIVITIES OF THE EARLY CHURCH:

a. Acts 2:42 describes four activities that the church did:

_____

_____

_____

_____

b. **Application Question**: How do you think that the church today follows their example? _____

_____

_____

6. THE KEY ISSUE OF FELLOWSHIP IS LOVE:

a. John 13:34-35 _____

b. 1 John 3:1 _____

7. WHAT DO WE DO WHEN WE FELLOWSHIP?

a. Hebrews 10:24-25 _____

b. Galatians 6:10 _____

c. Romans 15:25 _____

d. Romans 12:13 _____

e. Acts 17:11 _____

8. IS FELLOWSHIP AN OPTION FOR CHRISTIANS?

a. Hebrews 10:25 _____

b. What do you think some of the dangers of not having fellowship with other Christians might be for you?

_____

_____

_____

Assignment: Read Philippians, memorize Hebrews 10:25, and pray for one another.

Notes/Questions: _____

_____

_____

_____

The Holy Spirit

What blessing did you receive as a result of fellowship this week? _____

_____

THE HOLY SPIRIT, HIS DEITY AND PERSON

1. THE HOLY SPIRIT IS A PERSON:

    a. The Holy Spirit is not an impersonal force, power or influence. *He is a person.*

    b. The Bible uses personal pronouns in both the Greek and in English in speaking of Him – "He", "Him", etc.

    c. In John 14:16, who is the "He" referring to?

_____

2. HE DOES THINGS ONLY A PERSON CAN DO:

    a. John 14:26 _____

    b. Acts 13:2 _____

    c. John 16:8 _____

    d. Romans 8:14 _____

3. **BEING A PERSON, HE IS AFFECTED BY OUR ACTIONS AND ATTITUDES:**

   a. We can lie to Him – Acts 5:1-3.

   b. We can grieve Him – Ephesians 4:30.

   c. We can quench Him – 1 Thessalonians 5:19.

   d. We can insult Him – Hebrews 10:29.

4. **THE HOLY SPIRIT POSSESSES THE ATTRIBUTES OF GOD:**

   a. Omnipresent – Psalm 139:7-10.

   b. Omnipotent – Luke 1:35.

   c. Omniscient – John 14:26 and 16:12-13.

   d. Eternal – Hebrews 9:14.

   e. Holy – Romans 1:4.

   f. Creator – Job 33:4 and Psalm 104:30.

5. **HE IS DISTINCT FROM THE FATHER AND THE SON:**

   a. The Father, the Son and the Holy Spirit are each spoken of in Matthew 28:19.

   b. When Jesus was baptized, the Father spoke and sent the Holy Spirit to rest upon the Son – Luke 3:21-22.

6. **WHAT DOES THE HOLY SPIRIT DO WHEN WE ARE SAVED?**

   a. John 3:3-8 _____

   b. Titus 3:4-7 _____

   c. 1 Corinthians 3:16 & 6:19 _____

   d. John 7:37-39 _____

   e. Ephesians 1:13-14 _____

The Holy Spirit is recognized as God in Acts 5:3-4 and is active in man, convicting him of sin and guiding the believer into all truth as shown in John 16:5-15.

THE TRINITY

1. THE BIBLE TEACHES THAT THERE IS ONLY ONE GOD:

Read Deuteronomy 4:39 & 6:4, 2 Samuel 7:22, and Isaiah 43:10-13.

2. THE DOCTRINE OF THE TRINITY IS NOT EXPLICIT IN THE OLD TESTAMENT BUT IT IS IMPLIED:

Read and consider Genesis 1:26, 3:22 and 11:7.

3. IN GENESIS 1:1 THE HEBREW WORD FOR GOD IS PLURAL (ELOHIM):

    a. In Hebrew the singular word for God is "EL"

    b. In Hebrew the word for a dual God is "ELAH"

    c. In Hebrew the word for a plural (three or more) God is "ELOHIM"

4. THE EVIDENCES FOR THE TRINITY ARE EXPLICIT IN THE NEW TESTAMENT:

Read and consider Matthew 3:16-17, 1 Peter 1:2 and Jude 20-21.

5. THE SUMMARY:

    a. God is three persons (Father, Son and Holy Spirit).

    b. Each person is fully God.

    c. There is one God.

The Trinity is a difficult concept to grasp. Given the whole counsel of the Word of God, the Trinity is the only way we can explain the three persons of the Godhead. Even so, it is good to remember the words of Deuteronomy 29:29.

Assignment: Read John 14-17, memorize John 14:16, and pray for one another.

Notes/Questions: _____

_____

_____

_____

The Spirit-Filled Life, Part 1

In what way did you see the Holy Spirit at work in your life this week? _____

_____

THE SPIRIT-FILLED LIFE, PART 1

1. THE HOLY SPIRIT PLACES US INTO THE BODY OF CHRIST:

a. Whose body is it according to 1 Corinthians 12:27?

_____

b. Are all the members in a church body the same according to 1 Corinthians 12:14 & 17 and Romans 12:4-5?

_____

c. Who gives us our place in the body? See 1 Corinthians 12:18 and Ephesians 4:11-12

_____

d. According to 1 Corinthians 12:21-25 and 1 Peter 4:10, are we all needed in the body? _____

Why? _____

e. Do you need the other members of the body? See 1 Corinthians 12:21-26 _____

Why? _____

f. Who is the head of the body? See Colossians 1:18 and Ephesians 1:22 _____

2. THE HOLY SPIRIT GIVES EACH BELIEVER CERTAIN GIFTS AND ABILITIES:

Turn to 1 Corinthians 12:

a. According to verses 4-6, does everyone have the same gift? _____

b. Is there anyone who does not have at least one gift according to verse 7? _____

c. For whose benefit did God give these gifts?

_____

d. What are some examples of gifts in verses 8-10?

_____

_____

_____

e. Who chooses to give these gifts? (verse 11) _____

f. According to verse 31, what can we pray for?

_____

g. What is the greatest gift according to Paul in 1 Corinthians 13:13? _____

h. Paul makes some very strong statements in 1 Corinthians 13:1-3 concerning the importance of love. In these verses, which is the more important, using our gifts or *showing* love?_____

Why? _____

3. SUMMARY:

When you became a Christian, you immediately became a child of God, and were placed into a new spiritual family, the body of Christ. The human body functions best when each member fulfills the job it was created to perform. The body of Christ is much the same. It is healthiest when each member is growing spiritually and fulfilling their unique role.

Application Question: Where do I believe I fit in the Body of Christ? And, what should I be doing about it? _____

_____

_____

_____

Assignment: Read 1 Corinthians 12-14, memorize 1 Corinthians 13:13, and pray for one another.

Notes/Questions: _____

_____

_____

_____

The Spirit-Filled Life, Part 2

What does it mean to you that you are part of the body of Christ? _____

THE SPIRIT-FILLED LIFE, PART 2

1. THE PROMISE OF THE COMING OF THE HOLY SPIRIT:

   a. It was prophesied in the Old Testament – Joel 2:28-32

   b. It was promised by Jesus in the New Testament – John 14:16-17 & 26 and 15:26-27.

2. IN ACTS 1:4-5, WHAT DID JESUS TELL HIS DISCIPLES TO WAIT FOR? _____

3. TURN TO ACTS 1:8 AND CONSIDER THESE POINTS:

   a. The word "power" comes from the Greek work dunamis which also means "dynamite". Where does the power or ability to witness for Christ come from?

---

b. Before we were Christians the Holy Spirit was "with" (*para* in the Greek) us, convicting us of sin and drawing us to Christ. See John 16:8.

c. When we became Christians the Holy Spirit comes "in" (*en* in the Greek) us. See John 14:16-17 & 20:22 and 1 Corinthians 3:16.

d. The third experience of the Holy Spirit is when He comes "on" or "upon" (*epi* in the Greek) us and over-flows out of our life. See John 7:37-39.

   1) "Flow" in the Greek literally means to "gush forth".

   2) "Baptize" (*baptizo* in the Greek) means "over-flowed". We become a channel through which the Holy Spirit overflows to everyone around us.

   3) What happened in these examples of the Spirit coming upon a believer? Acts 10:44-46

_____

Acts 19:6_____

4. WHAT HAPPENS WHEN WE ARE BAPTIZED WITH THE HOLY SPIRIT?

a. We receive power to witness for Jesus and to serve Him in whatever area He asks us to.

b. We receive increased power to overcome sin.

c. The Scriptures come alive to us.

d. Our relationship with God is more alive and vital.

e. We receive spiritual gifts when we pray to God and ask for the baptism of the Holy Spirit. We receive it by faith (see Luke 11:9-13 and Galatians 3:2-5) just as we received Jesus Christ into our life by faith.

SHARING YOUR FAITH

1. ACCORDING TO 1 PETER 3:15, WHAT MUST HAP-
PEN IN OUR PERSONAL LIVES BEFORE WE ARE
READY TO SHARE OUR FAITH? _____

_____

2. WHAT DOES IT MEAN TO "SANCTIFY" THE LORD
IN OUR HEARTS? _____

_____

3. BASIC POINTS TO COVER IN SHARING YOUR FAITH:

a. All have sinned and fall short of the glory of God –
Romans 3:23.

b. The wages of sin is death – Romans 6:23.

c. God demonstrated His love to us by sending Jesus
Christ to die for us – Romans 5:8 and John 3:16.

d. We are saved by faith in Jesus Christ – Romans 10:9-10 &13.

e. Read and consider also these verses: Isaiah 59:1-2,
John 3:3, Acts 3:19-20 and Ephesians 2:8-9.

4. THE BASIC TOOLS FOR WITNESSING:

a. A Bible – a pocket-size New Testament is sufficient.

b. Tracts – these are widely available in Christian book-
stores. Use tracts that communicate well and that you
are comfortable with.

c. Memorize scripture. The above verses are a great place
to start.

5. REMEMBER:

a. The Holy Spirit is the One who will give you the words
and speak through you – Matthew 10:18-20.

b. The Lord is the One who adds to the church daily – Acts 2:47.

Assignment: Read the book of Acts, memorize Acts 1:8, and go put it into action!

Notes: _____

_____

_____

_____

_____

_____

_____

_____

_____

_____

_____

_____

_____

_____

_____

_____

_____

Notes: _____

_____

_____

_____

_____

_____

_____

_____

_____

_____

_____

_____

_____

_____

_____

_____

_____

_____

_____

_____

_____

_____